Genealogy
Standards

GENEALOGY STANDARDS

50TH ANNIVERSARY EDITION

Board for Certification of Genealogists
Post Office Box 14291
Washington, D.C. 20044
www.BCGcertification.org

 ancestry.com

Copyright © 2014
Board for Certification of Genealogists
P. O. Box 14291
Washington, D.C. 20044
Office@BCGcertification.org

Published by Ancestry.com,
an imprint of Turner Publishing Company
424 Church Street • Suite 2240 • Nashville, Tennessee 37219
445 Park Avenue • 9th Floor • New York, New York 10022

Genealogy standards
    p. cm.
Includes bibliographical references and glossary
ISBN 978-1-630-26018-7 (paper)
    1. Genealogists—Certification.
    2. Board for Certification of Genealogists (Washington, D.C.)—
    Handbooks, manuals, etc. I. Board for Certification of
    Genealogists (Washington, D.C.)
CS8.5 .B38 2013
929'.1–dc21

Printed in the United States of America.
14 15 16 17 18 19 0 1 2 3 4 5 6 7

CONTENTS

Chapter 4—
Standards for Writing................................ 31

CHAPTER 5—
STANDARDS FOR
GENEALOGICAL EDUCATORS 41

Chapter 6—
Standards for
Continuing Education

Appendix A—
The Genealogist's Code

Introduction

Accuracy is fundamental to genealogical research. Without it, a family's history would be fiction. This manual presents the standards family historians use to obtain valid results.

These standards apply to all genealogical research, whether shared privately or published. They also apply to personal research and research for clients, courts, and other employers. The standards address documentation; research planning and execution, including reasoning from evidence; compiling research results; genealogical education; and ongoing development of genealogical knowledge and skills.

Family historians throughout the twentieth century adapted concepts from the field of law to develop guidelines for assessing their research results. Recognizing flaws in attempting to apply one discipline's principles to another, from 1997 to 2000 the Board for Certification of Genealogists (BCG) clarified, organized, and compiled the field's best practices into the Genealogical

Proof Standard (GPS).[1] That effort led to *The BCG Genealogical Standards Manual,* released at the National Genealogical Society's annual conference in 2000.[2] That volume's contents have been the field's only published criteria for evaluating genealogical research processes and outcomes. Developed through deliberative collaborative efforts, those standards reflected a consensus among BCG's trustees, whose experience, peer-reviewed work samples and publications, and teaching place them among the field's leadership.

Since the first edition was published, genealogy has continued to advance, and its standards have continued to evolve, creating the need for a new edition. This edition—published in BCG's fiftieth year—updates, clarifies, consolidates, expands, and regroups the original standards. The revision also ties them more directly to the Genealogical Proof Standard. A new title reflects the standards' value for all genealogists.

Extensive rewording reflects changes since 2000, including technological and scientific advances. It also aims for greater clarity and stronger emphasis on family historians and their work. Refined definitions, now removed from the standards' content, appear in a glossary.

1. Helen F. M. Leary, "Evidence Revisited—DNA, POE, and GPS," *OnBoard: Newsletter of the Board for Certification of Genealogists* 4 (January 1998): 1–2 and 5.

2. Board for Certification of Genealogists, *The BCG Genealogical Standards Manual* (Orem, Utah: Ancestry, 2000).

The number of standards has increased from seventy-two to eighty-three. The increase, however, reflects reorganization more than added material. Sections of multipart standards now appear separately. The revision also groups related standards that previously appeared separately. For example, disparate documentation standards now appear together.

The reorganized standards fit into a modified overall structure. A new grouping, "Standards for Documenting," precedes other groupings because documentation applies to all phases of genealogical activity. Categories of research standards appear in the order in which genealogical researchers confront them: "Planning Research" (a new category), "Collecting Data" (formerly "Data-Collection"), and "Reasoning from Evidence" (formerly "Evidence-Evaluation"). New categories "Genealogical Proofs," "Assembled Research Results," and "Special-Use Genealogical Products" appear in a grouping of "Standards for Writing." They consolidate standards from "Compilation" (formerly under "Research Standards") with "Standards for Educational Writers" (formerly under "Teaching Standards").

Cross-references appended to many of the standards refer readers to the glossary for definitions related to the respective standard's content. The glossary includes terms and definitions that do not appear in a standard's wording and are not cross-referenced. These terms are relevant to genealogical standards and research.

Standards in this manual—as is typical of any field's standards—comprise two types:

- *Product standards* define qualities of useful outcomes.

- *Process standards* describe activities leading to useful outcomes.

This manual's standards are sensible and practical guidelines, not unreachable ideals. They describe processes that successful practitioners routinely implement. These standards address components of successful genealogical research and reasoning. They also address methods and formats for explaining genealogical reasoning and for sharing research results. Adhering to them leads to efficient genealogical research and effective outcomes.

BCG's trustees for 2011–12, 2012–13, and 2013–14 contributed to the manual's second edition. Their listing here acknowledges their commitment to high standards for the genealogical field, their work, and their contributions to this revision, all as volunteers:[3]

---

3. The terms and postnominals Certified Genealogist, CG, Certified Genealogical Lecturer, and CGL are service marks of the Board for Certification of Genealogists (BCG) used under license by certificants who meet genealogical competency standards prescribed for its programs. The board's name is registered with the United States Patent and Trademark Office. This manual's appendix A contains its code of ethics, and its appendix B provides additional information about BCG.

F. Warren Bittner, CG
Jeanne Larzalere Bloom, CG
Laura Murphy DeGrazia, CG
Victor S. Dunn, CG
Stefani Evans, CG
Ann Carter Fleming, CG, CGL
Kay Haviland Freilich, CG, CGL
Michael Grant Hait Jr., CG
Alison Hare, CG
Kay Germain Ingalls, CG
Thomas W. Jones, PhD, CG, CGL
Barbara Mathews, CG
David McDonald, CG
Debra S. Mieszala, CG
Elizabeth Shown Mills, CG, CGL
Elissa Scalise Powell, CG, CGL
Michael S. Ramage, JD, CG
Beverly Rice, CG
Christine Rose, CG, CGL
Judy G. Russell, JD, CG, CGL
Dawne Slater-Putt, CG
Willis H. White, CG

Donn Devine, JD, CG, who jump-started the revision by drafting revisions of many of the standards and leading online discussions of them, and Nicki Peak Birch, CG, contributed substantially to this edition. Public discussions on the Transitional Genealogists Forum, led and reported by Harold Henderson (now CG), also helped inform this revision. A second edition would not have been possible without the boundless dedication, effort, leadership, and vision that Helen F. M. Leary, CG,

CGL (now Certified Genealogist Emeritus), skillfully provided for the first edition.

The word *standard* has several conventional definitions, including "something set up and established by authority as a rule for the measure of quantity, weight, extent, value, or quality." Rather than a numerical measure, standards in this manual—like those for other advanced fields—perhaps more closely reflect another definition: "Something established by authority, custom, or general consent as a model or example: criterion."[4]

BCG offers these standards to the field as a guide to sound genealogical research and a way to assess the research outcomes that genealogists produce. They are standards for anyone who seeks to research and portray accurately people's lives, relationships, and histories.

Thomas W. Jones
Editor
October 2013

---

4. *Merriam-Webster's Collegiate Dictionary*, 11th ed. (Springfield, Mass.: Merriam-Webster, 2004), s.v. "standard" as a noun, definitions 3 and 4.

Chapter 1—The Genealogical Proof Standard

All genealogists strive to reconstruct family histories or achieve genealogical goals that reflect historical reality as closely as possible. They meet this goal by applying the Genealogical Proof Standard (GPS) to measure the credibility of conclusions about ancestral identities, relationships, and life events. The standard addresses completed research, not research in process. Overarching all of this manual's documentation, research, and writing standards, it has five interdependent components:

- Reasonably exhaustive research—emphasizing original records providing participants' information—for all evidence that might answer a genealogist's question about an identity, relationship, event, or situation

- Complete, accurate citations to the source or sources of each information item contributing—directly, indirectly, or negatively—to answers about that identity, relationship, event, or situation

- Tests—through processes of analysis and correlation—of all sources, information items, and evidence contributing to an answer to a genealogical question or problem

- Resolution of conflicts among evidence items pertaining to the proposed answer

- A soundly reasoned, coherently written conclusion based on the strongest available evidence

A genealogical conclusion is proved when it meets all five GPS components. Each part contributes to a proved conclusion's credibility:

- *Reasonably exhaustive research* ensures examination of all potentially relevant sources. It minimizes the risk that undiscovered evidence will overturn a too-hasty conclusion.

- *Complete and accurate source citations* demonstrate the research extent and sources' quality. They enable others to replicate the steps taken to reach a conclusion. (Inability to replicate research casts doubt on its conclusion.)

- *Critical tests of relevant evidence through processes of analysis and correlation* facilitate sound interpretation of information and evidence. They also ensure that the conclusion reflects all the evidence, including the best existing evidence.

- *Resolution of conflicting evidence* substantiates the conclusion's credibility. (If conflicting evidence is not resolved, a credible conclusion is not possible.)

- *Soundly reasoned, coherently written conclusion* eliminates the possibility that the conclusion is based on bias, preconception, or inadequate appreciation of the evidence. It also shows or explains how the evidence leads to the conclusion.[5]

Genealogical results cannot be partly proved. Proof results only when a genealogist's research, conclusion, and presentation of that conclusion reflect all five GPS components.

Genealogical proof rests on evidence from thorough examination of all known sources potentially relevant to solving a research problem. Genealogical proof reflects what that evidence shows after any conflicting evidence is resolved. Such proof, therefore, cannot be overturned by "might-have-beens." Possibilities for which no known evidence exists do not discredit a proved genealogical conclusion.

Meeting the GPS neither requires nor ensures perfect certainty. Genealogical proofs—like accepted conclusions in any research field—never are final. Previously unknown evidence may arise, causing the genealogist to reassess and reassemble the evidence, which may change the outcome.

---

5. Bullet points are adapted from "The Genealogical Proof Standard," *Board for Certification of Genealogists* (www.BCGcertific ation.org/resources/standard.html : 2013).

Chapter 2—Standards for Documenting

Documentation is fundamental to planning and executing genealogical research, collecting and recording data, and compiling research results. Documentation appears in working notes and shared genealogical-research outcomes. Shared materials include articles, blogs, charts and forms, family histories, lineage-society applications, and reports. Documentation also appears in educational materials for genealogists. The Genealogical Proof Standard requires complete and accurate citations to the source or sources of each information item supporting a claim that a conclusion is proved. Eight standards address genealogical documentation.

1. **Scope.** Genealogists use citations to identify the sources of all substantive information and images they gather, use, or plan to gather or use, except sources of "common knowledge" beyond dispute, such as the years of major historical events. [See glossary for definitions of CITATION, IMAGE, INFORMATION, and SOURCE.]

2. **Specificity.** Genealogists' citations connect one or more sources or information items with:

   - Each statement the genealogist makes that is someone else's observation, deduction, or opinion

   - Each fact that is not common knowledge

   - Each image the genealogist shows of someone else's creation

   - Each conclusion the genealogist establishes

   The specificity of these connections leaves no question about the basis or source of each statement, fact, image, or conclusion. [See glossary for definitions of CONCLUSION, IMAGE, and INFORMATION.]

3. **Purposes.** Citations, narrative text, and connections between the two enable genealogists and others to (a) assess the credibility of each source or image a genealogist used, (b) locate that source or image, and (c) understand the research scope. [See glossary for definitions of IMAGE and SOURCE.]

4. **Citation uses.** Genealogists place citations in research plans, logs, notes, works in progress, and similar materials. They use them in classroom and lecture materials. They also use citations, usually in footnotes, in all kinds of finished genealogical-research products, including articles, blogs, books, case studies, charts and forms, educational materials, family histories, other kinds of histories,

lineage-society applications, reports, and various kinds of written projects. [See glossary for the definitions of CITATION and FOOTNOTE.]

5. **Citation elements.** Complete citations use a standard format to describe at least four facets of each cited source:

- *Who*—the person, agency, business, government, office, or religious body that authored, created, edited, produced, or was responsible for the source; or, if identified, the source's informant

- *What*—the source's title or name; if it is untitled, a clear item-specific description

- *When*—the date the source was created, published, last modified, or accessed; in some cases if the source is unpublished, the date of the event it reports

- *Where*—if unpublished, the source's physical location; if a published book, CD-ROM, microfilm, or newspaper, its place of publication; if an online resource, a stable URL

Complete citations to information items documenting specific statements, facts, images, and conclusions (reference-note citations) describe a fifth facet:

- *Wherein*—the specific location within the source where the information item can be found, for example, page, image, or sequence number; or—if the source is unpublished—its box number, folder or collection name, or similar identifying information

[See glossary for definitions of CONCLUSION, IMAGE, INFORMANT, INFORMATION, PUBLISHED SOURCE, SOURCE, and UNPUBLISHED SOURCE.]

6. **Format.** Genealogists use humanities-style citations (notes plus bibliography), a style designed for heavy users of manuscript materials. They follow two guides modeling humanities-style principles and formats: *Evidence Explained* covers citations for a full array of materials used by genealogists;[6] *The Chicago Manual of Style* discusses capitalization, foreign languages, punctuation, and other documentation-related issues.[7] Other styles and systems are not standard for genealogical writing.[8] [See glossary for definitions of BIBLIOGRAPHY, DOCUMENT (*VERB*), and DOCUMENTATION.]

---

6. Elizabeth Shown Mills, *Evidence Explained: Citing History Sources from Artifacts to Cyberspace*, 2nd ed., revised (Baltimore: Genealogical Publishing Co., 2012). Also, digital edition available at *Evidence Explained: Historical Analysis, Citation, and Source Usage* (https://www.evidenceexplained.com/ : 2013), via "Book Store."

7. *The Chicago Manual of Style*, 16th ed. (Chicago: University of Chicago Press, 2010).

8. Nonstandard styles for genealogical writing include scientific style (parenthetical short-form references, like *The Chicago Manual*'s "Author-Date References" system) and other disciplines' styles and formats, like those of the American Psychological Association (APA), Associated Press (AP), and Modern Language Association (MLA).

7. **Shortcuts.** Once they cite a source completely, genealogists may use a short-form citation or "ibid.," when appropriate, to refer back to a complete citation documenting the source of a statement, fact, image, or conclusion in the same finished product or in the same section of a finished product. [See glossary for definitions of DOCUMENT (*VERB*), IMAGE, and SHORT-FORM CITATION.]

8. **Separation safeguards.** When transmitting or storing documented material, genealogists prevent mechanical or digital separation of citations from the statements, facts, images, and conclusions they document. Such safeguards may include placing metadata or images in digital files, citations on the fronts of photocopied material, uniquely numbered footnotes at the bottoms of pages corresponding to superscripts in narrative text on the same pages, page numbering showing both page number and total pages, and reference notes, endnotes, and photocopies on firmly attached pages. [See glossary for definitions of DOCUMENT (*VERB*), ENDNOTE, FOOT-NOTE, IMAGE, and REFERENCE NOTE.]

Chapter 3—Standards for Researching

Planning Research

Planned research avoids inefficiency, needless reexamination of sources, omission of useful sources, and other pitfalls of haphazard examination of source material. Ten standards address genealogical research planning.

9. **Planned research.** Genealogical research begins with and follows dynamic plans for gathering information from—or images of—resources. The plan's purpose is to meet stated objectives, usually in the form of research questions. [See glossary for definitions of INFORMATION, RESEARCH QUESTION, and SOURCE.]

10. **Effective research questions.** Questions underlying research plans concern aspects of identity, relationship, events, and situations. The questions are sufficiently broad to be answerable with evidence from relevant places and times. They are sufficiently focused to yield answers that may be tested and shown to meet or not to meet the Genealogical

Proof Standard. Genealogical-research questions include (a) a clearly described unique person, group, or event as the question's focus; and (b) specification of unknown or forgotten information that the research is to discover (for example, an identity, relationship, event, or biographical detail). [See glossary for definitions of EVIDENCE, GENEALOGICAL PROOF STANDARD, IDENTITY, RELATIONSHIP, and RESEARCH QUESTION.]

11. **Sound basis.** Research plans seek unknown or forgotten information about a specific person, family, group, event, or situation. Plans begin with analyzing starting-point information for accuracy. Plans also avoid assumptions about people and events that documentation does not support. [See glossary for definitions of ACCURATE, ANALYSIS, DOCUMENT (*VERB*), DOCUMENTATION, and INFORMATION.]

12. **Broad context.** When planning research, genealogists consider historical boundaries and their changes, migration patterns and routes, and sources available for potentially relevant times and places. They also consider economic, ethnic, genetic, governmental, historical, legal, linguistic, military, paleographic, religious, social, and other factors that could affect the research plan and scope.

13. **Source-based content.** Research plans list all types of sources likely to provide or lead to evidence that

helps meet a plan's objective. Plans may list databases, finding aids, indexes, search engines, and other mechanisms for accessing sources. Research plans also may include authored narratives, derivative records, and documented and undocumented genealogies. Wherever possible, however, research plans follow such materials to original records and primary information. [See glossary for definitions of AUTHORED NARRATIVE, DERIVATIVE RECORD, DOCUMENT (*VERB*), EVIDENCE, INFORMATION, ORIGINAL RECORD, PRIMARY INFORMATION, RECORD (*NOUN*), and SOURCE.]

14. **Topical breadth.** Genealogists plan to consult sources naming or affecting their research subjects and their relatives, neighbors, and associates. Their plans often include artifacts, authored narratives, oral histories, various kinds of records, and other sources concerning agriculture, demographics, DNA, economies, ethnicities, geography, government, history, inheritance, land, laws, migration, military activity, occupations, social customs and norms, religions, or other aspects of the research questions under investigation. [See glossary for definitions of AUTHORED NARRATIVE, RECORD (*NOUN*), and SOURCE.]

15. **Efficient sequence.** Research plans specify the order for examining resources. These sequences give priority to efficient discovery of useful evidence. [See glossary for definition of EVIDENCE.]

16. **Flexibility.** Genealogical research plans may initially comprise only one or a few resources. As genealogists follow the plan, materials they examine might (a) not provide the expected information, (b) provide unexpected information, or (c) suggest further resources to examine. Consequently, genealogists repeatedly add to or otherwise modify their research plans. [See glossary for definition of SOURCE.]

17. **Extent.** Whether a genealogical question is simple or complex, the research plan aims for "reasonably exhaustive" research, required for genealogical proof. Thorough research gathers sufficient data to test—and to support or reject—hypotheses concerning identities, relationships, events, and situations. Acquiring sufficient data may require broadening the research beyond the person, family, event, or situation in question. Thorough research attempts to gather all reliable information potentially relevant to the research question, including evidence items conflicting or consistent with other evidence items. Thorough research, therefore, aims to consult all potentially relevant sources. It emphasizes original records containing primary information, which may be used as direct, indirect, or negative evidence. [See glossary for definitions of CONFLICTING EVIDENCE, DIRECT EVIDENCE, EVIDENCE, EXHAUSTIVE RESEARCH, INDIRECT EVIDENCE,

INFORMATION, NEGATIVE EVIDENCE, ORIGINAL RECORD, PRIMARY INFORMATION, PROOF, REASONABLY EXHAUSTIVE RESEARCH, RECORD (NOUN), RELATIONSHIP, RESEARCH QUESTION, and SOURCE.]

18. **Terminating the plan.** In ideal situations, genealogists continue searching until they have sufficient evidence for a defensible answer to their plan's underlying research question. If necessary, however, they may terminate a plan before acquiring sufficient evidence. (For example, they may have expended time, financial, or other resources available to implement the plan or know of no further resources to consult.) Genealogists understand that terminating a plan that has yielded insufficient evidence for a defensible answer will not lead to genealogical proof. [See glossary for definitions of EVIDENCE, PROOF, RESEARCH QUESTION, and SOURCE.]

Collecting Data

The Genealogical Proof Standard requires thorough research related to the identity, relationship, event, or situation in question. Genealogists collect information from a variety of sources, and about widely diverse subjects, in order to understand the identity, history, and relationships of a particular person, family, or group. Eighteen standards address genealogical data-collection activities.

19. **Data-collection scope.** Genealogists attempt to collect all information potentially relevant to the questions they investigate. [See glossary for definitions of INFORMATION and RESEARCH QUESTION.]

20. **Careful handling.** Genealogists treat all source materials and images of source materials carefully, with regard for their preservation and future availability. [See glossary for definitions of IMAGE and SOURCE.]

21. **Respect for source caretakers.** Genealogists interact courteously with administrators, archivists, curators, librarians, and other caretakers or custodians of source materials and information. Genealogists respect these professionals' roles in preserving materials and information and making them available to researchers. [See glossary for definitions of INFORMATION and SOURCE.]

22. **Using others' work.** Genealogists ethically, lawfully, prudently, and respectfully use others' information and products, whether the material is digitized, oral, published, unpublished, written, or in any other form. Their data collection includes (a) providing full attribution to the originator, (b) accurately representing the originator's information, and (c) honestly assessing the information's nature and significance. [See glossary for definitions of ACCURATE, INFORMATION, PUBLISHED SOURCE, and UNPUBLISHED SOURCE.]

23. **Reading handwriting.** Genealogists correctly read all legible handwriting in materials they consult.

24. **Understanding meanings.** Genealogists correctly understand the meaning of all legible words, phrases, and statements in the sources they consult. Their understanding includes the meaning for the source's time and place.

25. **Note-taking content.** When examining sources, genealogists cite them and make notes about their contents and features of potential relevance to the investigation. These notes include content, formatting, and other features:

    • Physical features and contextual cues, including any indication the source may be damaged, incomplete, or incorrectly dated

    • Names, dates, places, circumstances, and other content, exactly as they appear in the source material

    • Formatting, headings and subheadings, column headings, digital-source metadata, notations on the front or back of a page or appended to it, explanatory text (whether or not adjacent to the source or item of interest), footnotes and endnotes, and amendments and emendations

[See glossary for definitions of ENDNOTE, FOOTNOTE, and SOURCE.]

26. **Distinction between content and comments.** Genealogists' notes clearly distinguish abstracted, quoted, and transcribed source content from their own comments, descriptions, interpretations, paraphrases, and summaries of that content.

27. **Note-taking objectivity.** Genealogists do not allow bias, preference, or preconception to affect their choices of information to collect and not to collect. They suspend judgment about the information's effect on the research question until after they have collected sufficient relevant information, analyzed it, and compared it to other findings. [See glossary for definitions of ANALYSIS, INFORMATION, and RESEARCH QUESTION.]

28. **Images and printouts.** Data collection includes scanning and photographing text, images, and artifacts for later use or study or to show handwriting, engraving, layout, or other relevant aspects of a source's appearance. Images and printouts include the entire source or the entire item of interest. Genealogists attach citations to images and printouts, and they protect images and printouts from alteration. [See glossary for definitions of CITATION and IMAGE.]

29. **Transcriptions.** Genealogists transcribe to show or study a modern-print version of a document, record, or source. Transcriptions include the entire item—including any headings, insertions, notations,

endorsements, or the like—whether on the item's front or back or on an attachment. When formatting is relevant to a transcription's use, the transcription reflects the transcribed item's format, layout, line lengths, and other physical features. Genealogists identify the transcription's beginning and end. Annotations between square brackets or in footnotes or separate text show where a source is damaged or illegible, omits expected information, or provides unexpected information. [See glossary for definitions of FOOTNOTE, INFORMATION, RECORD (NOUN), and SOURCE.]

30. **Abstracts.** Abstracts omit redundant, repetitive, and formulaic wording in the abstracted record and judiciously smooth out the remaining text. Genealogists use quotation marks or indented formatting to identify any phrases of three or more words appearing in the original. They do not modernize names or dates. Otherwise, abstracts adhere to the standard for transcriptions. [See glossary for definition of RECORD (NOUN).]

31. **Quotations.** Genealogists quote or extract to capture definitive, confusing, colorful, or unusual phrases. They also quote or extract to show or study a modern-print version of a written source's part or parts. Genealogists identify quoted material by placing it between quotation marks or in an indented, block-quotation format. Following current *Chicago Manual of Style* guidelines, genealogists use ellipsis

points to replace words they omit from quotations. Genealogists' selections of quotations and omissions within them do not alter the original writer's meaning. [See glossary for definition of RECORD (*NOUN*).]

32. **Transcribing, abstracting, and quoting principles.** Genealogists cite the source of all transcribed, abstracted, and quoted material. When quoting and transcribing, genealogists render wording, spelling, numbering, abbreviations, superscripts, and similar features exactly as they appear in the original. Except at the beginnings and ends of quotations, genealogists also show capitalization and punctuation exactly as they appear in the original. Genealogists transcribe obsolete letter forms with their modern equivalents or with the original letter form, if it is in their character set; they do not substitute modern look-alikes with a different meaning (for example *f* for the long *s*, *y* for the thorn, *ff* for capital *F*, or *sc* for *x*). Genealogists may add short insertions to transcriptions, abstracts, and quotations by placing them between square brackets. Longer commentary appears before or after the transcription, abstract, or quotation as clearly marked separate text or as one or more attached footnotes or endnotes. [See glossary for definitions of ENDNOTE and FOOTNOTE.]

33. **Paraphrases and summaries.** In their working notes and finished products genealogists may paraphrase or summarize a source's content, if the

result explains the original material without altering its meaning. Genealogists source-cite paraphrases and summaries. They place quotation marks around any phrases of three or more words that appear in the original.

34. **Agents.** Genealogists may use agents to find and examine sources, make images from them, and provide the images directly to the genealogist—or otherwise to find, obtain, and provide information potentially relevant to a research question. Providing clear directions, genealogists specify what the agent is to supply. When an agent does not provide complete images, genealogists ask them for commentary sufficient to ensure correct interpretation of the source and its context. In their works in progress and finished products, genealogists acknowledge their agents' roles. [See glossary for definitions of CONCLUSION, IMAGE, INFORMATION, and RESEARCH QUESTION.]

35. **Source analysis.** As they examine potentially relevant sources, genealogists appraise each source's likely accuracy, integrity, and completeness. This appraisal considers the source's characteristics:

- Physical condition

- Legibility

- Whether it is an original or derivative record or an authored narrative

- The source's internal consistency—how parts of the source agree or disagree with each other

- The source's external consistency—how it compares with other items in the same series or collection

- The source's history, including its governance, provenance, purpose, recorder, storage, and time lapse between events and their recordation

[See glossary for definitions of ACCURATE, ANALYSIS, AUTHORED NARRATIVE, DERIVATIVE RECORD, ORIGINAL RECORD, PROVENANCE, RECORD (*NOUN*), and SOURCE.]

36. **Information analysis.** As they collect potentially relevant information items from sources, genealogists appraise each item's likely accuracy, integrity, and completeness. This appraisal considers each item's characteristics:

- Legibility

- Who provided the information

- That person's reliability and consistency as witness and as reporter

- Whether the information is primary or secondary, or undetermined

- The information item's internal consistency—the presence or absence of contradictions within the item

- The item's external consistency—how it compares with other information in the same source

[See glossary for definitions of ACCURATE, ANALY-SIS, INFORMATION, PRIMARY INFORMATION, SECONDARY INFORMATION, and UNDETERMINED.]

Reasoning from Evidence

The Genealogical Proof Standard requires genealogists to base conclusions on reliable evidence from independent information items. A conclusion's soundness rests on (a) assessments of each relevant source and information item and (b) genealogists' abilities to reason from the evidence that those sources and information items provide. Fourteen standards address reasoning from evidence.

37. **Sources, information, and evidence.** Genealogists view sources as containers of information items potentially relevant to research questions. They use the information items as evidence of answers to those research questions. [See glossary for definitions of EVIDENCE, INFORMATION, RESEARCH QUESTION, and SOURCE.]

38. **Source preference.** Whenever possible, genealogists prefer to reason from original records that reliable scribes carefully created soon after the reported events. They also prefer original records that competent authorities checked or vetted and that institutions maintained with protections from alteration, damage, and tampering. At the same

time, genealogists understand that some preferred sources could be proved inaccurate, less desirable sources might be proved accurate, or less desirable sources may be the only extant relevant sources. [See glossary for definitions of ACCURATE, ORIGINAL RECORD, RECORD (*NOUN*), and SOURCE.]

39. Information preference. Whenever possible, genealogists prefer to reason from information provided by consistently reliable participants, eyewitnesses, and reporters with no bias, potential for gain, or other motivation to distort, invent, omit, or otherwise report incorrect information. At the same time, genealogists understand that some preferred information items could be proved inaccurate, less desirable items might be proved accurate, or they may be the only extant relevant information items. [See glossary for definitions of ACCURATE and INFORMATION.]

40. Evidence mining. Genealogists obtain evidence from information items and sets of information items. They seek evidence items that answer research questions directly, indirectly, or negatively. Evidence mining requires attention to detail, including details that might initially seem insignificant. Genealogists ignore no potentially useful evidence—including indirect and negative evidence or evidence that might conflict with or complicate a working hypothesis—and they give equal attention to direct, indirect, and negative evidence. [See glossary for definitions of CONFLICTING EVIDENCE,

DIRECT EVIDENCE, EVIDENCE, HYPOTHESIS, INDIRECT
EVIDENCE, INFORMATION, NEGATIVE EVIDENCE, and
RESEARCH QUESTION.]

41. **Evidence scope.** Genealogists obtain much of
their evidence from information naming people of
interest or their possible relatives, neighbors, and
associates. Genealogists also obtain useful evidence
from sources that do not name these people. These
include histories of the area, its population, and relevant time periods, and works describing customs,
governance, laws, and regulations. [See glossary for
definitions of EVIDENCE and INFORMATION.]

42. **Evidence discrimination.** Genealogists include
in their reasoning all known sources and information items that seem relevant to a research question.
They exclude all sources and information items that
seem irrelevant to that question. To ensure that their
reasoning identifies all known relevant evidence,
genealogists examine their justifications for including and excluding sources and information items.
They are prepared to defend those justifications.
[See glossary for definitions of EVIDENCE, INFORMA-
TION, RESEARCH QUESTION, and SOURCE.]

43. **Evidence integrity.** Genealogists do not trim, tailor, slight, or ignore potentially relevant evidence to
fit a bias or preconception, to harmonize with other
evidence, or for any other reason. [See glossary for
definition of EVIDENCE.]

44. Evidence reliability. Genealogists recognize that any seemingly relevant evidence item may be proved reliable or not reliable. They understand that unreliable evidence may be useful, for example, to follow as a clue, explain an error, or resolve conflicting evidence. [See glossary for definitions of CONFLICTING EVIDENCE, EVIDENCE, and RESOLUTION.]

45. Assumptions. As they obtain evidence, genealogists recognize their assumptions, categorize them, and differentially address each kind of assumption:

- *Fundamental assumptions* are concepts generally accepted as true. (For example, people do not act after their deaths or before their births; travel between places is consistent with the period's technology.) Genealogists incorporate fundamental assumptions into their reasoning.

- *Valid assumptions* are concepts generally accepted as true unless convincingly contradicted. (For example, mothers between twelve and forty-nine years old conceive children; personal behavior and life patterns are coherent; people generally observed the legal, moral, and social standards of their time and place.) Genealogists seek evidence to invalidate such assumptions. If they cannot find such evidence, they incorporate the assumptions into their reasoning.

- *Unsound assumptions* are concepts that may be valid but cannot be accepted without supporting evidence. (For example, a man's widow was the mother of his children; migrating families followed popular routes; a bride's surname is that of her parents.) Genealogists seek evidence to support such assumptions. If they find it, the assumption becomes valid. If they cannot find supporting evidence, they do not incorporate the unsound assumption into their reasoning.

[See glossary for definition of EVIDENCE.]

46. **Evidence independence.** Genealogists weigh evidence from independent information items. When information items are related (for example, birthdate information from an obituary and death certificate with the same informant), genealogists weigh them only after grouping the related items into a unit. Then they assign that unit no more credibility than the weight of the group's strongest item. [See glossary for definitions of EVIDENCE, INDEPENDENT INFORMATION ITEMS, INFORMANT, INFORMATION, PRIMARY INFORMATION, and RELATED INFORMATION.]

47. **Evidence correlation.** Genealogists test their evidence by comparing and contrasting evidence items. They use such correlation to discover parallels, patterns, and inconsistencies, including points at which evidence items agree, conflict, or both. [See glossary for definitions of CONFLICTING EVIDENCE, CORRELATION, and EVIDENCE.]

48. **Resolving evidence inconsistencies.** Genealogists attempt to resolve conflicts or incompatibilities among two or more evidence items. Resolution

involves (a) identifying evidence items that support each side of a conflict and (b) articulating a defensible rationale for setting aside evidence items that support all but one side of the conflict. Defensible rationales include showing—after all known relevant evidence is considered—that (a) only one uncorroborated evidence item or only one combination of related evidence items supports one side, (b) showing that significantly more error-prone sources and information items support one side, (c) explaining why evidence for one side is substantially less credible than evidence for the other side, or (d) any combination of rationales a–c. [See glossary for definitions of COMPATIBLE EVIDENCE, CONFLICTING EVIDENCE, EVIDENCE, INFORMATION, RELATED INFORMATION, and RESOLUTION.]

49. **Unresolved evidence inconsistencies.** Genealogists understand that not all conflicting evidence can be resolved and that, in such circumstances, a conclusion cannot be proved. [See glossary for definitions of CONFLICTING EVIDENCE, EVIDENCE, and RESOLUTION.]

50. **Assembling conclusions from evidence.** Once a genealogist resolves conflicting evidence, all remaining relevant evidence items are compatible with a single answer to the research question. This answer becomes a conclusion. Credible conclusions may rest on direct, indirect, or negative evidence in any combination. Credible conclusions include

placing individuals accurately in their families or other groups. [See glossary for definitions of ACCU-RATE, COMPATIBLE EVIDENCE, CONCLUSION, CONFLICT-ING EVIDENCE, DIRECT EVIDENCE, EVIDENCE, INDIRECT EVIDENCE, NEGATIVE EVIDENCE, RESEARCH QUESTION, and RESOLUTION.]

Chapter 4—Standards for Writing

Genealogical Proofs

The Genealogical Proof Standard requires a written conclusion. Genealogists, therefore, write proofs. (Sources and citations are not genealogical proofs.) Depending on the complexity of the genealogist's research question and the evidence supporting its answer, the proof may take the form of a proof statement, proof summary, or proof argument. Four standards address genealogical proofs.

51. Research scope. Clear and accurate source citations and narrative text supporting genealogical proofs show three qualities:

- The underlying research was reasonably thorough.

- The genealogist used all sources and information items that competent genealogists would use to support the conclusion.

- Where possible, the genealogist used original records and primary information items.

[See glossary for definitions of ACCURATE, CONCLU-
SION, INDEPENDENT INFORMATION ITEMS, INFORMA-
TION, ORIGINAL RECORD, PRIMARY INFORMATION, PROOF
ARGUMENT, PROOF STATEMENT, PROOF SUMMARY, REA-
SONABLY EXHAUSTIVE RESEARCH, RECORD (NOUN), and
RESEARCH QUESTION.]

52. **Proved conclusions.** Genealogical proofs show
accurate answers to research questions. Proofs may
specify the question, or the answer may imply the
question. [See glossary for definitions of ACCURATE,
CONCLUSION, PROOF, and RESEARCH QUESTION.]

53. **Selection of appropriate options.** Genealogists
select the proof option appropriate for the proved
conclusion's context:

- *Proof statements* are source-cited sentences and data
  items in thoroughly documented contexts demonstrating adequate research scope. Genealogists use
  proof statements when at least two citations demonstrate that a conclusion's accuracy requires no
  explanation. Proof statements usually appear in
  documented presentations of genealogical research
  results, including articles, blogs, case studies, chap-
  ters, charts, family histories, monographs, reports,
  tables, and other printed and online works.

- *Proof summaries* are relatively straightforward narratives or lists with documentation. Genealogists use
  proof summaries when the evidence is direct and
  any conflicts are minor. Proof summaries require
  no more than a few paragraphs or a few pages to

provide a rationale for a conclusion's accuracy and explain the resolution of any evidence conflicting with that conclusion. Proof summaries may stand alone or accompany a report, image, or lineage-society application. They also may appear in a broader context—for example, within an article or case study, a narrative family history or monograph, or a report for a client, court, or personal files.

- *Proof arguments* are extensive documented narratives that often include figures, tables, or other enhancements. Genealogists use proof arguments to explain challenging cases, especially those where thorough research reveals significant conflicts between evidence items or an absence of direct evidence. Proof arguments may stand alone—comprising, for example, an article, blog post, or case study. They also may appear within a broader context—for example, a narrative family history or monograph, or a report for a client, court, or personal files.

[See glossary for definitions of ACCURATE, CONCLUSION, CONFLICTING EVIDENCE, DIRECT EVIDENCE, DOCUMENT (*VERB*), DOCUMENTATION, EVIDENCE, IMAGE, PROOF, PROOF ARGUMENT, PROOF STATEMENT, PROOF SUMMARY, and RESOLUTION.]

54. **Logical organization.** Proof summaries and arguments present data, discussions, and conclusions in logical sequences to explain or defend a research question's answer. A logical sequence often is not the order in which the genealogist collected evidence or reached subsidiary conclusions. [See glossary for

definitions of CONCLUSION, EVIDENCE, PROOF ARGU-
MENT, PROOF SUMMARY, and RESEARCH QUESTION.]

Assembled Research Results

Genealogists assemble research results into family histories, lineages, narrative genealogies, and pedigrees.
They also present research outcomes in articles, blogs,
case studies, charts and forms, kinship-determination
projects, narrative histories, and other written products and projects. Twelve standards address assembled
research results.

55. Integrity and ownership. Genealogical writers
observe all ethical and legal standards that safeguard
against plagiarism and copyright infringement.
Genealogists take special care when paraphrasing
and quoting to avoid (a) assuming credit for others'
words and ideas and (b) misrepresenting others'
ideas or intent. Genealogists secure the owner's
permission to use or reuse copyrighted or privately
owned material.

56. Honesty. All genealogical writings present evidence
objectively and without bias or preconception.
They do not distort, mask, overplay, or underplay
evidence. [See glossary for definition of EVIDENCE.]

57. Background information. Assembled research
results provide sufficient background information

for readers to understand both what an information item says and what it means in the context of each source's place and time and in the context of the written presentation. Background information may include concepts from economics, ethnic studies, genetics, geography, government, history, law, religion, sociology, and other fields. [See glossary for definition of INFORMATION.]

58. **Content.** Assembled genealogical-research results discuss or show the information's reliability and its relevance to the research questions underlying the reported research. Discussions, figures, lists, tables, or a combination show how the evidence correlates. If evidence conflicts, the discussion explains how the genealogist resolved the conflict or why it could not be resolved. [See glossary for definitions of CONFLICTING EVIDENCE, CORRELATION, EVIDENCE, INFORMATION, RESEARCH QUESTION, and RESOLUTION.]

59. **Proofs included.** Assembled genealogical-research results include—as appropriate for the context— proof statements, proof summaries, proof arguments, or any combination. [See glossary for definitions of PROOF, PROOF ARGUMENT, PROOF STATEMENT, and PROOF SUMMARY.]

60. **Overall format.** Genealogists design page layout, typeface, headings, and other aspects of physical appearance to maximize intelligibility of their data,

discussions, interpretations, analyses, and conclusions. [See glossary for definitions of ANALYSIS and CONCLUSION.]

61. **Structure.** Genealogists organize written presentations and discussions of assembled research results into structured parts and logical sequences.

62. **Clear writing.** Genealogical writing meets general conventions for accuracy, clarity, and coherence. Written narratives are reasonably free from abbreviations, chitchat, convolutions, dead-end arguments, digressions, extraneous details, jargon, malapropisms, typographical errors, and other characteristics that interfere with readability. Writing style is straightforward and precise. [See glossary for definition of ACCURATE.]

63. **Technically correct writing.** Genealogists' capitalization, grammar, spelling, punctuation, and word usage follow widely accepted conventions and rules.

64. **Cross referencing.** Assembled research results include call-outs or cross-references to all enhancements and supplementary material, including audio and video recordings, digital images, figures, illustrations, maps, photocopies, photographs, scans, and tables. [See glossary for definition of IMAGE.]

65. **Genealogical formats.** As a part of assembled genealogical-research results, or as the presentation

in its entirety, genealogists have three formatting options for showing family relationships:[9]

- *Genealogies* show descent from one person or couple. At least one generation in a genealogy highlights more than one couple or family. Genealogies use either *NGSQ*-system or *Register*-system formatting and numbering.

- *Lineages* show descent from one person or couple or ascent from one person. Lineages highlight only one person, couple, or family in each generation. They need not be numbered.

- *Pedigrees* show ascent from one person. At least one generation in a pedigree highlights more than one couple or family. Pedigrees use the Sosa-Stradonitz ahnentafel-based numbering system.

[See glossary for definition of AHNENTAFEL, GENE-ALOGY, and RELATIONSHIP.]

66. **Biographical information.** Genealogies, pedigrees, lineages, and most other genealogical writing include descriptive biographical narrative besides any vital statistics. These details include sufficient information about each person's or family's activities, residences, circumstances, contributions, and

---

9. For detailed descriptions and illustrations of genealogical formats, see Joan Ferris Curran, Madilyn Coen Crane, and John H. Wray, *Numbering Your Genealogy: Basic Systems, Complex Families, and International Kin,* NGS special publication no. 97, edited by Elizabeth Shown Mills (Arlington, Va.: National Genealogical Society, 2008).

lifestyle to identify them uniquely within the context of their historical era, society, and geographic place.

Special-Use Genealogical Products

Genealogists prepare written products for specific uses or users. These products include seven categories: reports, lineage-society applications, source guides, methodology guides, compiled abstracts, reviews, and database programs. Besides applicable documentation, research, and other writing standards, seven standards address, respectively, these seven kinds of products.

67. Reports. Stand-alone reports of genealogical-research results include at least nine parts or characteristics:

- Identification of the report writer and any intended recipients, preparation date, and topic

- Sufficient recapitulation of prior research to put the reported research in its broader context

- Purposes or focuses of the report, or specifications by intended recipients (usually a paying or pro bono client or employer) of the report's goal, scope, format, and delivery

- Any restrictions on research hours, repository or source access, expenses, or other resources

- Content and format, including legally dictated form and phrasing for some law-related genealogical reports, focused on the report's stated purposes and specifications, including well-reasoned explanations of why any research goal or purpose was or was not met

- Context and background of the planned research (for example, missing records, multiple people of the same name, inaccurate prior compilations)

- Presentation of findings by source, name, date, place, significance, or other scheme that is appropriate to the findings or research project, that sequences the findings clearly and logically, and that provides sufficient detail to avoid unnecessary future searches of the same records

- Descriptions of searches that do not yield evidence (along with findings of direct, indirect, and negative evidence, which all genealogical-research products provide) in sufficient detail to avoid unnecessary future searches of the same records

- Safeguards to minimize risks of alteration and loss or separation of any part of the report

[See glossary for definitions of ACCURATE, DIRECT EVIDENCE, EVIDENCE, INDIRECT EVIDENCE, NEGATIVE EVIDENCE, NEGATIVE SEARCH, and RECORD (NOUN).]

68. **Lineage-society applications.** Applications for lineage-society membership adhere to the society's instructions.

69. Source guides. Guides to genealogical source materials provide sound directions and information about materials within the guide's scope.

70. Methodology guides. Guides to genealogical methods provide clear, explicit instructions in logical progressions. They provide written and visual examples that are precisely on point, clarify the process, and enhance learning.

71. Compiled abstracts. Compilers do not alphabetize abstracts or arrange them differently from the source. Compilers may, however, rearrange data within abstracts to follow a consistent format, but only when rearrangement does not alter or obscure any original meaning.

72. Reviews. Reviews of genealogical books and other media provide analysis that is concise, balanced, and impartial. They are based on sufficient reading or use of the product and sufficient background for a valid judgment of the material's accuracy, reliability, usability, and validity. [See glossary for definition of ACCURATE.]

73. Database programs. Genealogical database programs do not require users to attempt conclusions prematurely, tailor findings to any limitation a program may have, or bypass any documentation, research, or writing standard.

Chapter 5—Standards for Genealogical Educators

Lecturers and Instructors

Genealogical educators may be lecturers, instructors, or both. Lecturers present focused instructional sessions at genealogical conferences, seminars, webinars, workshops, and other educational events. Instructors present courses—a series of interrelated classes—on one or more genealogical topics. Lecturers and instructors may deliver education in person or via electronic media. Eight standards address genealogical education.

74. **Planned outcomes.** Genealogical educators plan classes, courses, lectures, and other presentations to facilitate student acquisition of genealogical knowledge, genealogical skills, or both.

75. **Content titles.** Genealogical educators provide class, course, lecture, and presentation titles that reflect their planned outcomes and are useful for the intended audience.

76. **Enhancements.** Handouts, slides, and any other class, lecture, and presentation enhancements

provide accurate, up-to-date information appropriate for the class or lecture topic. The materials adhere to this manual's documentation standards, and they supplement the class, lecture, or presentation without detracting from it. [See glossary for definitions of ACCURATE, DOCUMENT (*VERB*), and DOCUMENTATION.]

77. **Bibliographies.** Handouts include up-to-date bibliographies that are suitable for the topic.

78. **Presentation style.** Genealogical educators deliver well-organized, clearly articulated, and up-to-date classes, lectures, presentations, and other instructional activities leading to the planned outcomes. Class presentations encourage student participation.

79. **Ownership.** Genealogical educators develop their own materials, including bibliographies, class activities, handouts, and presentations. They use any part of another person's material only with written permission and written and oral attribution to the material's developer.

80. **Course design.** Teachers sequence activities, classes, and topics to develop student knowledge, skills, or both in a cohesive, logical order.

81. **Student evaluation.** Genealogical courses include activities enabling teachers to assess each student's attainment of the planned course outcomes.

Chapter 6—Standards for Continuing Education

Knowledge and Skill Development

Like all research fields, the genealogy field grows and changes. Like all researchers, genealogists must advance with their field and continually improve their knowledge and skill. Two standards address genealogists' knowledge and skill development.

82. **Development goals.** Genealogists improve and update their (a) attainment of genealogical standards, (b) knowledge of genealogically useful materials and contexts, (c) skills in reconstructing unknown or forgotten relationships, families, people, groups, and events, and (d) abilities to present their findings to others. [See glossary for definitions of PROOF and RELATIONSHIP.]

83. **Regular engagement.** Genealogists engage in formal or informal development activities, or both, on an ongoing basis:

   • Formal development activities include attending conference, seminar, and workshop presentations in person or via electronic media; participating in classroom-based or online courses of study; and engaging in virtual or in-person structured study groups, webinars, and similar venues. Development activities via electronic media may occur either when the event is live or afterward; participation with others may be in real time or asynchronous.

- Informal development activities include conducting genealogical research of increasing difficulty, consulting with advanced practitioners, critiquing other genealogists' work, mentoring or teaching genealogists, studying the field's peer-reviewed research journals, and subjecting written materials to expert critiques.

Appendix A—
The Genealogist's Code

In 1964 BCG's founding trustees developed and disseminated the field's first ethics code, addressing the relationship between genealogical practitioners and beneficiaries of their work. In 1994 the board updated the code to reflect changes in copyright law and the effect of electronic media on research and reporting techniques, but its basic principles are unchanged.

All BCG-certified genealogists sign a statement saying "I . . . do hereby acknowledge that I concur with the code of ethics set forth by the Board for Certification of Genealogists and that I shall follow its standards in all phases of my work as a genealogist." Whether board-certified or not, all reputable genealogists abide by the code's provisions. It addresses the three major areas of genealogical enterprise in the following words:

To protect the public

- I will not publish or publicize as fact anything I know to be false, doubtful, or unproved; nor will

I be a party, directly or indirectly, to such action by others.

- I will identify my sources for all information and cite only those I have personally used.

- I will quote sources precisely, avoiding any alterations that I do not clearly identify as editorial interpretations.

- I will present the purpose, practice, scope, and possibilities of genealogical research within a realistic framework.

- I will delineate my abilities, publications, and/or fees in a true and realistic fashion.

To protect the consumer (client or colleague)

- I will keep confidential any personal or genealogical information given to me, unless I receive written consent to the contrary.

- I will reveal to the consumer any personal or financial interests that might compromise my professional obligations.

- I will undertake paid research commissions only after a clear agreement as to scope and fee.

- I will, to the best of my abilities, address my research to the issue raised by the consumer and report to that question.

- I will seek from the consumer all prior information and documentation related to the research and will not knowingly repeat the work as billable hours without explanation as to good cause.

- I will furnish only facts I can substantiate with adequate documentation; and I will not withhold any data necessary for the consumer's purpose.

- If the research question involves analysis of data in order to establish a genealogical relationship or identity, I will report that the conclusions are based on the weight of the available evidence and that absolute proof of genealogical relationships is usually not possible.

- If I cannot resolve a research problem within the limitations of time or budget established by contract, I will explain the reasons why.

- If other feasible avenues are available, I will suggest them; but I will not misrepresent the possibilities of additional research.

- I will return any advance payment that exceeds the hours and expenses incurred.

- I will not publish or circulate research or reports to which a client or colleague has a proprietary right, without that person's prior written consent; I will observe these rights, whether my report was made directly to the consumer or to an employer or agent.

To protect the profession

- I will act, speak, and write in a manner I believe to be in the best interests of the profession and scholarship of genealogy.

- I will participate in exposing genealogical fraud; but I will not otherwise knowingly injure or attempt to injure the reputation, prospects, or practice of another genealogist.

- I will not attempt to supplant another genealogist already employed by a client or agency. I will substitute for another researcher only with specific, written consent of and instructions provided by the client or agency.

- I will not represent as my own the work of another. This includes works that are copyrighted, in the public domain, or unpublished. This pledge includes reports, lecture materials, audio/visual tapes, compiled records, and authored essays.

- I will not reproduce for public dissemination, in an oral or written fashion, the work of another genealogist, writer, or lecturer without that person's written consent. In citing another's work, I will give proper credit.

Appendix B—About the Board for Certification of Genealogists

BCG is an active and integral part of the genealogical community. Its mission is to promote the highest standards of competence and ethics among genealogists and thereby foster public confidence in genealogy as a respectable and respected research discipline and field of study.

Since its founding in 1964 by leading American genealogists, BCG has viewed genealogical study as an avocation, profession, vocation, and social science that requires education and advanced skill, regardless of where or how the genealogist shares research results, and whether or not the genealogist accepts payment for research, teaching, or other services.

Besides BCG's certification program, it expresses its commitment to education through programs of publication and teaching.

Publications

In addition to this manual, BCG publishes print and online materials:

- *The BCG Application Guide* sets out requirements and procedures for applying for BCG certification. The guide is a PDF, downloadable at no charge from www.BCGcertification.org.

- *OnBoard*, BCG's educational newsletter, is published every four months. It carries articles about the Genealogical Proof Standard, genealogical sources, and issues concerning genealogical research and researchers. BCG certificants and preliminary applicants receive *OnBoard* as part of their fee; others may subscribe to it.

- *Board for Certification of Genealogists* is BCG's public-access website, located at www.BCGcertification.org. It provides educational materials, work samples, articles from back issues of *OnBoard*, information about applying for BCG certification, a guide to genealogical education, and a searchable roster of BCG certificants.

- *Springboard*, at blog.BCGcertification.org, is BCG's blog. It provides news of the board and its certificants.

- BCG's pamphlets describe aspects of genealogical research and the process of applying for BCG certification.

EducATioNAl AcTiviTiEs

BCG cosponsors, provides, and supports genealogical education activities:

- BCG cosponsors the Institute of Genealogy and Historical Research—IGHR (Samford University Library; 800 Lakeshore Drive; Birmingham, AL 35229; www.samford.edu/schools/ighr/index.html). Launched in 1965, IGHR annually offers an assortment of academically and professionally oriented week-long courses at Samford University. The faculty is composed of outstanding genealogical educators of national and international repute.

- BCG is a trustee of the National Institute on Genealogical Research—NIGR (Post Office Box 118; Greenbelt, MD 20786-0118). Founded in 1950, NIGR is based at the National Archives in Washington, D.C., and College Park, MD. It offers an intensive one-week course of study focused on archived federal records of genealogical value.

- BCG supports skill-building tracks at annual conferences of national scope. The tracks typically comprise about fifteen in-depth classes or lectures focused on intermediate and advanced genealogical-research topics.

- BCG also sponsors lectures and seminars at national, regional, and local meetings and events. These presentations typically focus on genealogical standards and BCG certification.

- In 2000 BCG founded the BCG Education Fund, an independent nonprofit charitable trust that advances BCG's educational aims by (a) funding learning programs consistent with BCG standards and (b) providing incentives for study and scholarly research in accordance with BCG standards.

CERTIFICATION PROGRAM

Since 1964 BCG has administered a certification program that provides valid skill assessment, consumer protection, and respected credentials. This manual's standards provide the basis for that evaluation.

Via mail or online, applicants submit a portfolio of work samples demonstrating that their research, reasoning, and reporting skills meet those standards. The 2014 edition of *The BCG Application Guide* specifies four kinds of work samples:

- A transcription, abstract, analysis, and research plan for both a BCG-supplied and an applicant-supplied document

- A report of research findings prepared for someone who does not share the applicant's own, in-laws', or children's ancestry

- A case study solving a complex problem for which thorough research reveals significantly conflicting evidence or an absence of direct evidence

- A narrative genealogy, lineage, or pedigree describing, documenting, and linking individuals, couples, and families through at least three generations

Applicants also sign The Genealogist's Code and provide a biographical résumé.

Three to four judges use standardized rubrics to objectively evaluate the work samples. Each applicant receives ratings and written feedback. Applicants whose work samples meet the standards achieve an unbiased endorsement of their competence as genealogical researchers and writers. Applicants who have submitted premature applications may utilize their evaluation feedback and reapply.

For further information about the applicant work samples, submission and judging processes, fees, and other details, see *The BCG Application Guide*.

Organizational Structure

BCG fills three roles:

- An independent organization, not affiliated with or part of any society or group

- A certifying body, not a membership society

- A nationally and internationally recognized standards organization

The board consists of fifteen trustees, a professional executive director, and a panel of approximately forty-five judges. BCG certificants annually elect five trustees to three-year terms. The trustees annually elect BCG's president, vice president, secretary, and treasurer and a member-at-large of the executive committee. All trustees, officers, and judges are BCG-certified, and they serve without compensation.

The BCG trustees meet annually in the fall, usually in October in Salt Lake City. They hold additional meetings during the year, often in conjunction with a national conference in the spring.

BCG's bylaws are a public document published on the board's website. See *Board for Certification of Genealogists* (www.BCGcertification.org/brochures/BCGBylaws Revised2013.pdf : 2013).

BCG's Addresses:

- Board for Certification of Genealogists
  Post Office Box 14291
  Washington, D.C. 20044

- Office@BCGcertification.org

- www.BCGcertification.org

Appendix C—Sources and Resources

Source Material and Related Readings

Bell, Mary McCampbell. "Transcripts and Abstracts." In *Professional Genealogy: A Manual for Researchers, Writers, Editors, Lecturers, and Librarians*, edited by Elizabeth Shown Mills. Baltimore: Genealogical Publishing Company, 2001.

Board for Certification of Genealogists. *The BCG Genealogical Standards Manual*, millennium edition. Orem, Utah: Ancestry, 2000.

"Certification: Frequently Asked Questions (FAQ)." *Board for Certification of Genealogists*. www .BCGcertification.org/certification/faq.html: 2013.

The Chicago Manual of Style, 16th edition. Chicago: University of Chicago Press, 2010.

Curran, Joan Ferris, Madilyn Coen Crane, and John H. Wray. *Numbering Your Genealogy: Basic Systems, Complex Families, and International Kin*, NGS special publication no. 97, edited by Elizabeth Shown Mills. Arlington, Virginia: National Genealogical Society, 2008.

DeGrazia, Laura A. "Skillbuilding: Proof Arguments." *OnBoard: Newsletter of the Board for Certification of Genealogists* 15 (January 2009): 1–3.

Devine, Donn. "Evidence Analysis." In *Professional Genealogy: A Manual for Researchers, Writers, Editors, Lecturers, and Librarians,* edited by Elizabeth Shown Mills. Baltimore: Genealogical Publishing Company, 2001.

"Educational Preparation." *Board for Certification of Genealogists.* www.BCGcertification.org/certification/educ.html : 2013.

Evans, Stefani. "Data Analysis." *OnBoard: Newsletter of the Board for Certification of Genealogists* 18 (May 2012): 13–14.

———. "Correlation of Evidence." *OnBoard: Newsletter of the Board for Certification of Genealogists* 18 (September 2012): 21–23.

"The Genealogical Proof Standard." *Board for Certification of Genealogists.* www.BCGcertification.org/resources/standard.html : 2013.

"How to Become Certified." *Board for Certification of Genealogists.* www.BCGcertification.org/certification/index.html : 2013.

Jones, Thomas W. "Focused Versus Diffuse Research." *OnBoard: Newsletter of the Board for Certification of Genealogists* 17 (September 2011): 17–18.

————. "The Genealogical Proof Standard: How Simple Can It Be?" *OnBoard: Newsletter of the Board for Certification of Genealogists* 16 (September 2010): 17–18 and 20.

————. *Mastering Genealogical Proof.* Arlington, Virginia: National Genealogical Society, 2013.

Leary, Helen F. M. "Evidence Revisited—DNA, POE, and GPS." *OnBoard: Newsletter of the Board for Certification of Genealogists* 4 (January 1998): 1–2 and 5.

————. "Problem Analyses and Research Plans." In *Professional Genealogy: A Manual for Researchers, Writers, Editors, Lecturers, and Librarians,* edited by Elizabeth Shown Mills. Baltimore: Genealogical Publishing Company, 2001.

Leary, Helen F. M., Elizabeth Shown Mills, and Christine Rose. "Evidence Analysis." In *1999 NGS Conference in the States: Richmond, Virginia,* program syllabus. Arlington, Virginia: National Genealogical Society, 1999.

Little, Barbara Vines. "Skillbuilding: It's Not That Hard to Write Proof Arguments." *OnBoard: Newsletter of the Board for Certification of Genealogists* 15 (September 2009): 20–23.

Merriman, Brenda Dougall. *Genealogical Standards of Evidence: A Guide for Family Historians.* Toronto: Dundurn Press, 2010.

Mills, Elizabeth Shown. *Evidence Explained: Historical Analysis, Citation, and Source Usage.* www.evidence explained.com : 2013.

————. *Evidence Explained: Citing History Sources from Artifacts to Cyberspace*, 2nd edition, revised. Baltimore: Genealogical Publishing Company, 2012. Also, digital edition available from *Evidence Explained: Historical Analysis, Citation, and Source Usage* (www.evidenceexplained.com : 2013), via "Book Store."

————. "Research Reports" and "Proof Arguments and Case Studies." In *Professional Genealogy: A Manual for Researchers, Writers, Editors, Lecturers, and Librarians*, edited by Elizabeth Shown Mills. Baltimore: Genealogical Publishing Company, 2001.

————. "Working with Historical Evidence: Genealogical Principles and Standards." *National Genealogical Society Quarterly* 87 (September 1999): 165–84.

"Publications." *Board for Certification of Genealogists.* www.BCGcertification.org/catalog/index .html : 2013.

Rose, Christine. *Genealogical Proof Standard: Building a Solid Case*, 3rd edition. San Jose, California: CR Publications, 2009.

Resources for Examples

The American Genealogist, a quarterly journal privately published in Demorest, Georgia. [This publication and similar journals of record publish in every issue case studies and narrative genealogies meeting genealogical standards.]

Board for Certification of Genealogists. *The BCG Genealogical Standards Manual*, millennium edition. Orem, Utah: Ancestry, 2000. [Appendixes in this edition provide fictitious genealogical reports and narratives exemplifying BCG standards.]

"The Donald Lines Jacobus Award." *American Society of Genealogists.* fasg.org/awards/jacobus-award/ : 2013. [The web page lists publications that have won the Jacobus award, which the American Society of Genealogists established in 1972 to encourage sound scholarship in genealogical writing. Each winning entry demonstrates the highest genealogical standards in use when it received the award.]

Family History Writing Contest winning entries. [The National Genealogical Society sponsors an annual competition for genealogical narratives that span at least three generations, demonstrate genealogical standards, and develop human interest. The *National Genealogical Society Quarterly* publishes the winning entries, usually in the December issue. For contest details, see "Family History Writing Contest," *National Genealogical Society* (www.ngsgenealogy.org/cs/family_history_writing_contest : 2013).]

The Genealogist, twice yearly publication of the American Society of Genealogists, Boxford, Massachusetts. [This publication and similar journals of record publish in every issue case studies and narrative genealogies meeting genealogical standards.]

National Genealogical Society Quarterly, publication of the National Genealogical Society, Arlington, Virginia. [Every issue of the *Quarterly* contains case studies demonstrating and explaining the successful application of genealogical standards to solve complex problems.]

New England Historical and Genealogical Register, quarterly publication of the New England Historic Genealogical Society, Boston. [This publication and similar journals of record publish in every issue case studies and narrative genealogies meeting genealogical standards.]

New York Genealogical and Biographical Record, quarterly publication of the New York Genealogical and Biographical Society, New York. [This publication and similar journals of record publish in every issue case studies and narrative genealogies meeting genealogical standards.]

"Sample Work Products." *Board for Certification of Genealogists*. www.BCGcertification.org/skillbuilders/worksamples.html : 2013. [The BCG website provides an assortment of case studies and proof arguments of various lengths. Each exemplifies genealogical standards.]

Appendix D—
Glossary

Many of this glossary's definitions reflect specialized genealogical usages beyond the defined terms' ordinary dictionary meanings.

accurate

A term applied to genealogical sources, information, evidence, and conclusions, and to proof statements, proof summaries, and proof arguments when the GPS shows they portray identities, relationships, and events as they were in the past or are today; compare with *prove;* see *Genealogical Proof Standard*

ahnentafel

A genealogical numbering system in which a compiler assigns

Note: This glossary, modified from Thomas W. Jones, *Mastering Genealogical Proof* (Arlington, Va.: National Genealogical Society, 2013), 133–40, is adapted and used here with permission of its author and publisher.

number *1* to a subject, *2* to the subject's father, *3* to the subject's mother, and continues by using double each person's number for that person's father and double the person's number plus *1* for that person's mother

analysis

The recognition of information and evidence items a source contains that are likely to answer a research question directly, indirectly, or negatively; also, a consideration of the characteristics, purpose, and history of a source and its relevant information items in order to determine their likely accuracy

authored narrative

A written product that synthesizes information from many prior sources and presents the writer's own conclusions, interpretations, and thoughts; one of three kinds of genealogical *source;* compare with *record*

bibliography

See s*ource list*

citation

A source reference that uses a standard format to describe the source

compatible evidence

Evidence items that agree even if differing in detail (for example, *Molly* and *Mary* may be variants of the same name); the opposite of *conflicting evidence*

conclusion

An answer to a research question that has passed tests of analysis and correlation but has not been explained or stated in writing and documented; also, a recapitulation of a proof summary or proof argument that states or restates what the summary or argument has proved

conflicting evidence

Evidence items that could not all be correct (for example, Molly could not have been born in both Georgia and New York); the opposite of *compatible evidence*

correlation

A process of comparing and contrasting genealogical information and evidence to reveal conflicts, parallels, and patterns

derivative record

A record created from a prior record by (a) transcribing the prior record or part of it by hand or keyboard or by using optical-character-recognition, speech-to-text, or other technology, (b) abstracting information from it, (c) translating it from one language to another, or (d) reproducing it with alterations; also, a work created to expand accessibility to the prior record's information, or to some part of it; the opposite of *original record* and one of three kinds of genealogical *source;* see *record*

direct evidence

An information item that seems to address a research question and answer it by itself; the opposite of *indirect evidence* and one of three categories of genealogical *evidence*

discursive note

A reference note containing discussion, usually along with one or more citations; see *reference note* document (*verb*)

The processes of recording and showing the sources of concepts, evidence, images, and words that an author or compiler has used

documentation

The sources supporting genealogical conclusions and proof, citations to those sources, the genealogist's comments about them, and formatting showing the connections between the sources and specific statements and conclusions

endnote

A reference note placed at the end of an article, book, report, web publication, or other genealogical work to document a statement within the work; see *reference note*; compare with *footnote*

evidence

A research question's tentative answer, which may be right or wrong, complete or incomplete, or vague or specific; may be *direct, indirect,* or *negative*

exhaustive search	A search that examines all sources, an impossible task; see *reasonably exhaustive research*
facsimile	An image showing a source with no sign of cropping, blurring, or other alteration, including color or shading changes that mask information; an exact copy; see *image*
first reference note	See *long-form citation*
footnote	A reference note appearing at the bottom of a page to document a statement on that page; see *reference note;* compare with *endnote*
full reference note	See *long-form citation*
Genealogical Proof Standard (GPS)	The genealogy field's standard for determining whether a conclusion is acceptable or not
genealogy	A research field concerned primarily with accurately reconstructing forgotten or unknown identities and familial relationships in the past and present,

typically covering more than one generation and including adoptive, biological, extramarital, marital, and other kinds of familial relationships; also, a narrative family history covering descendants of an ancestral couple

GPS

See *Genealogical Proof Standard*

hypothesis

Evidence or a potential conclusion subjected to tests of accuracy; see *evidence* and *conclusion*

identity

Characteristics and contexts distinguishing one person from all other people throughout history

image

A film, photocopy, photograph, scan, video, or other replication of a physical source; compare with *facsimile*

independent information items

Sources or information items that have unrelated origins, thus reinforcing rather than duplicating each other; sometimes called "independent sources"; the opposite of *related information*

indeterminable   See *undetermined*

indirect evidence   Information items that seem to address and answer a research question only when combined; the opposite of *direct evidence* and one of three categories of genealogical *evidence*

informant   A person who provided one or more information items; see *information*

information   Statements arising from experience, fabrication, hearsay, intuition, observation, reading, research, or some other means; or a source's surface content, including its physical characteristics; what we see or hear when we examine a source, not what we interpret; may be *primary*, *secondary*, or *undetermined*

long-form citation   A sentence-style format used for a written work's first citation to a particular source and providing all applicable citation details; compare with *short-form citation*; see *citation*

medium	A means of showing facsimiles or images of physical sources, including digital images, film, microfiche, microfilm, photocopies, photographs, and video; see *facsimile*, *image*, and *physical source*
negative evidence	A type of evidence arising from an absence of a situation or information in extant records where that information might be expected; one of three categories of genealogical *evidence*; compare with *negative search*
negative search	A search that does not yield useful evidence; compare with *negative evidence*
original record	A report of an action, observation, utterance, or other event, often but not always made at the time of the event or soon after and not based on a prior record; the opposite of *derivative record* and one of three kinds of genealogical *source*; see *record*

physical source	A source that can be held or touched but also may be viewed via a *medium;* see *image* and s*ource*
primary information	A report of an event or circumstance by an eyewitness or participant; the opposite of *secondary information*
proof	A documented statement, summary, or argument that explains or shows why a conclusion is proved; also, a description of a genealogical conclusion that is acceptable because it meets the Genealogical Proof Standard's five components
proof argument	A documented narrative that explains why a genealogist's answer to a complex genealogical problem should be considered acceptable and which may either be a stand-alone product (like a case study, journal article, or report) or appear within a chapter, family history, or other genealogical work in print, online, or elsewhere

proof statement

A documented data item or sentence stating an acceptable conclusion within a genealogical article, blog, chapter, chart, family history, report, table, or other work in print, online, or elsewhere containing documentation that demonstrates research scope sufficient to support the statement's accuracy; see *accurate*

proof summary

A documented narrative or list stating facts that support or lead to an acceptable conclusion and which may be a standalone product, may accompany an image, collection of images, or lineage-society application, or may appear in an article, blog, chapter, narrative family history, report, or other genealogical work in print, online, or elsewhere

prove

The process of using the GPS to show that a conclusion portrays identities, relationships, and events as they were in the past or are today; to establish that a genealogical conclusion is acceptable or accurate; see *accurate*

provenance

The history of a source's custody

published source

A source made available for distribution to people wishing a copy; the opposite of *unpublished source*

reasonably exhaustive research

A Genealogical Proof Standard component, requiring research thorough enough to meet five criteria: (a) yield at least two sources of independent information items agreeing directly or indirectly on a research question's answer, (b) cover sources competent genealogists would examine to answer the same research question, (c) provide at least some primary information and direct, indirect, or negative evidence from at least one original record, (d) replace, where possible, relevant authored narratives, derivative records, and information that is secondary or undetermined, and (e) yield, where possible, data from sources that indexes and databases identify as potentially relevant

record (*noun*)

An account, in a fixed medium (usually written but may also be fixed by audio or video recording, photography, or other means), of an action, observation, utterance, or other event, typically intended to describe, document, memorialize, or note the action, observation, utterance, or other event; may be *original* or *derivative*; a broad subcategory of genealogical *source*

reference list

See *source list*

reference note

A numbered paragraph-style feature of scholarly writing that contains one or more citations documenting a specific fact, statement, or series of statements bearing the same number, superscripted, as the reference note; a generic term covering *footnote* and *endnote*; see *discursive note*

related information	Information items that can be traced to one informant, source, or origin; therefore items that duplicate, rather than reinforce, each other; sometimes called "related sources"; the opposite of *independent information items*
relationship	A connection between events, evidence, information, or people
repository	An agency, building, or room housing source material, like an archive (personal, private, or public), courthouse, historical society, library, museum, town hall, or office (business, governmental, personal, religious, or other use)
research	An investigation designed to discover or interpret facts and thus to advance knowledge
research question	A question that research aims to answer; in genealogy a focused question that seeks unknown information about a specific person and that helps frame research scope, lead to relevant information, and identify evidence

resolution

The separation of conflicting or incompatible answers to a research question into likely correct and likely incorrect evidence, the discard of the likely incorrect evidence, and the explanation for the separation and rationale(s) for the discarding; see *conflicting evidence*

secondary information

A report by someone who obtained the information from someone else; hearsay; the opposite of *primary information*

short-form citation

A sentence-style format used for all but a work's first citation to a particular source and providing only enough detail to trigger recall and identification of the prior long-form citation and to document the statement to which it is attached; see *long-form citation*

short note

See *short-form citation*

source

A container of information; includes all kinds of publications and unpublished artifacts, records, recordings, and written materials; may be used in a *physical* form or as a *facsimile*; may be classified as an *original record, derivative record,* or *authored narrative*

source list

An alphabetical or categorical grouping of citations showing research scope, providing the general documentary basis for the content of a lecture, lesson, presentation, or written work, or directing others to sources related to such content

source-list citation

A paragraph-style format, customarily with a hanging indent, used to identify a source fully but not to document a specific statement, and typically not including reference to a specific item within a source

standard

A principle or measure of quality established by an authority

subsequent note

See *short-form citation*

undetermined

A description of information items that cannot be classified as primary or secondary, because

either the informant is unknown
or the genealogist cannot determine how a known informant
obtained the information

unpublished source   A source for which only one or
a few copies exist, or a source
for which distribution is limited
to select people or places; the
opposite of *published source*

Evidence Analysis
A Research Process Map

Basic Principle:

SOURCES provide INFORMATION
from which we identify EVIDENCE for ANALYSIS.
A sound CONCLUSION may then be considered "PROOF."

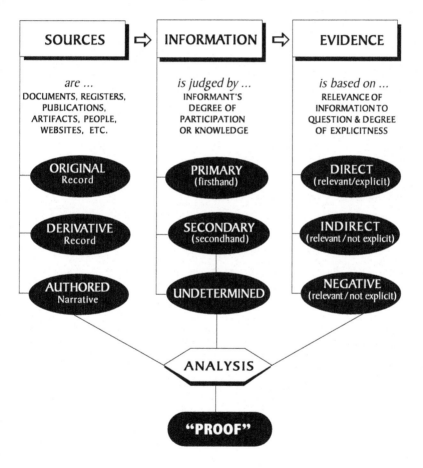

SOURCES	INFORMATION	EVIDENCE
are ...	*is judged by ...*	*is based on ...*
DOCUMENTS, REGISTERS, PUBLICATIONS, ARTIFACTS, PEOPLE, WEBSITES, ETC.	INFORMANT'S DEGREE OF PARTICIPATION OR KNOWLEDGE	RELEVANCE OF INFORMATION TO QUESTION & DEGREE OF EXPLICITNESS
ORIGINAL Record	PRIMARY (firsthand)	DIRECT (relevant/explicit)
DERIVATIVE Record	SECONDARY (secondhand)	INDIRECT (relevant / not explicit)
AUTHORED Narrative	UNDETERMINED	NEGATIVE (relevant / not explicit)

ANALYSIS

"PROOF"

CPSIA information can be obtained at www.ICGtesting.com
Printed in the USA
BVOW06s0628101115

426530BV00035B/507/P